Welcome to
Wealth:

The Ultimate Wealth Building Journal.

This Journal will help you to get your finances in order. It includes monthly prompts, budgeting form, checklists, quotes, affirmation, tips, and so many other wealth building resources to help you along the way. Use this Journal to help you accomplish your financial goals and gain wealth.

Dr. Synovia
CEO of A2Z Books Publishing

What is the Secret to Wealth you might ask?

The Answer is Gratitude, because if you are Grateful for what you have you are the Richest Person!

Tony Robbins

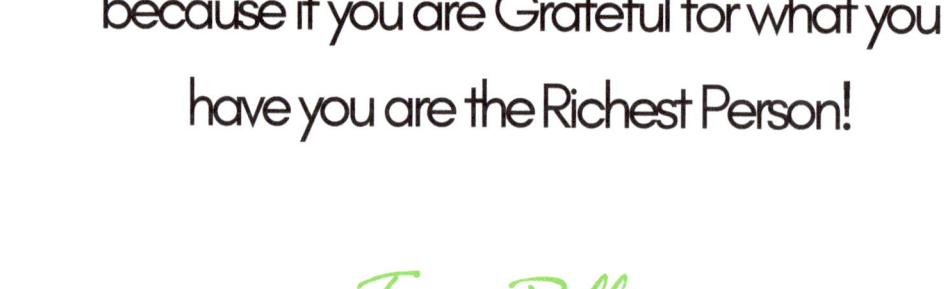

Printed in the USA by A2Z Books, LLC.
Copyright by Dr. Synovia Dover-Harris of A2Z Books Publishing.
All rights reserved. This book or any portion thereof may not be reproduced
or used in any manner whatsoever without the express
written permission of the publisher except for the use of brief
quotations in book review Printed in the United States.
First Printing
ISBN 978-1-943284-92-4
www.A2ZBookspublishing.net

This Wealth Building Journal Belongs to:

_____

_____

_____

Wealth is not about having a lot of money; it's about having a lot of options.

Chris Rock

Google defines Wealth as
" wealth "
/welTH/

an abundance of valuable possessions or money.
"he used his wealth to bribe officials"

I am going to Define Wealth as
(Define wealth for yourself here).

_____

_____

_____

_____

_____

Am I Wealthy?
___ Yes
___ No

If I answered yes, how do I know I am Wealthy?

_____
_____
_____
_____
_____

If I answered no, what changes do I need to make to make sure I am building Wealth?

_____
_____
_____
_____
_____

Wealth is the product of man's capacity to think.

Ayn Rand

Wealth Building Checklist:

(Check all of the items you currently have)

- [ ] I have a Savings Account
- [ ] I own Real Estate
- [ ] I own my car
- [ ] My investments are diversified
- [ ] I have little to no credit card debt
- [ ] I have an Emergency fund
- [ ] I have and follow my Budget
- [ ] I live below my means
- [ ] I have multiple streams of income
- [ ] I have investments
- [ ] I have stocks and bonds
- [ ] I have a retirement account
- [ ] My income is diversified

Write down the items you do not currently have from the wealth building checklist:

_____
_____
_____
_____
_____

What is your Plan to obtain these items?

_____
_____
_____
_____
_____

Assets

as•set
/ aset/

Defined as a useful or valuable thing, person, or quality. Property owned by a person or company, regarded as having value and available to meet debts, commitments, or legacies.

List All of Your Assets Here:

1. _____
2. _____
3. _____
4. _____
5. _____
6. _____
7. _____
8. _____
9. _____
10. _____

Debt/
/det/
Li•a•bil•i•ty
/ˌlīəˈbilədē/

Is defined as money, that is owed or due.

List Your All of Debt & Liabilities Here:

1. _____
2. _____
3. _____
4. _____
5. _____
6. _____
7. _____
8. _____
9. _____
10. _____

What are your plans to pay off this

1. _____
2. _____
3. _____
4. _____
5. _____

FINANCIAL GOALS

What are my Financial Goals for Next 6 months?
(List Financial Goals Here)

1. _____
2. _____
3. _____
4. _____
5. _____

What are my Financial Goals for Next 12 months?
(List Financial Goals Here)

1. _____
2. _____
3. _____
4. _____
5. _____

What are my Financial Goals for Next 5 Years?
(List Financial Goals Here)

1. _____
2. _____
3. _____
4. _____
5. _____

What am I going to do to achieve these goals?

1. _____
2. _____
3. _____
4. _____
5. _____
6. _____
7. _____
8. _____
9. _____
10. _____

What are my Biggest Financial Fears?
(List your Financial Fears Here)

_____

_____

_____

_____

_____

_____

_____

_____

_____

_____

_____

_____

_____

_____

_____

_____

Monthly Wealth Checklist

How much money do I have in my Checking Account?

How much money do I want in my Checking Account by the end of the month?

How much money do I have in my Savings Account?

How much money do I want in my Savings Account by the end of the month?

How much money do I want in my Retirement Account by the end of the month?

Monthly Budget

Monthly Spending _____

SUN	MON	TUE	WED	THU	FRI	SAT

BILL AND EXPENSE TRACKER

Monthly Bill Checklist _____

- ☐ _____
- ☐ _____
- ☐ _____
- ☐ _____
- ☐ _____

- ☐ _____
- ☐ _____
- ☐ _____
- ☐ _____
- ☐ _____

BILLS PAID _____

BILLS DUE _____

PURCHASE TRACKER

ITEM PURCHASED	STORE	AMOUNT

ITEM PURCHASED	STORE	AMOUNT

Write & Recite:

I am a Money Magnet

_____

_____

What is my relationship and thoughts about money?
(Journal your relationship with Money Here)

There are people who have money and people who are rich.

Coco Chanel

Monthly Wealth Checklist

How much money do I have in my Checking Account?

How much money do I want in my Checking Account by the end of the month?

How much money do I have in my Savings Account?

How much money do I want in my Savings Account by the end of the month?

How much money do I want in my Retirement Account by the end of the month?

Wealth Building Tip

Build an Emergency Fund

Monthly Budget

Monthly Spending _____

SUN	MON	TUE	WED	THU	FRI	SAT

BILL AND EXPENSE TRACKER

Monthly Bill Checklist _____

- ☐ _____
- ☐ _____
- ☐ _____
- ☐ _____
- ☐ _____

- ☐ _____
- ☐ _____
- ☐ _____
- ☐ _____
- ☐ _____

BILLS PAID _____

BILLS DUE _____

PURCHASE TRACKER

ITEM PURCHASED	STORE	AMOUNT	ITEM PURCHASED	STORE	AMOUNT

Write & Recite:

Wealth Flows into my life

_____

_____

What is my relationship and thoughts about money?
(Journal your relationship with Money Here)

A bank is a place that will lend you money if you can prove that you don't need it.

Bob Hope

Monthly Wealth Checklist

How much money do I have in my Checking Account?

How much money do I want in my Checking Account by the end of the month?

How much money do I have in my Savings Account?

How much money do I want in my Savings Account by the end of the month?

How much money do I want in my Retirement Account by the end of the month?

Wealth Building Tip
Pay off Credit Cards

Monthly Budget

Monthly Spending _____

SUN	MON	TUE	WED	THU	FRI	SAT

BILL AND EXPENSE TRACKER

Monthly Bill Checklist _____

- ☐ _____   ☐ _____
- ☐ _____   ☐ _____
- ☐ _____   ☐ _____
- ☐ _____   ☐ _____
- ☐ _____   ☐ _____

BILLS PAID _____

BILLS DUE _____

PURCHASE TRACKER

ITEM PURCHASED	STORE	AMOUNT

ITEM PURCHASED	STORE	AMOUNT

Write & Recite:

I am aligned with Wealth

_____

_____

What is my relationship and thoughts about money?
(Journal your relationship with Money Here)

That money talks, I'll not deny, I heard it once:
It said, 'Goodbye'.

Richard Armour

Monthly Wealth Checklist

How much money do I have in my Checking Account?

How much money do I want in my Checking Account by the end of the month?

How much money do I have in my Savings Account?

How much money do I want in my Savings Account by the end of the month?

How much money do I want in my Retirement Account by the end of the month?

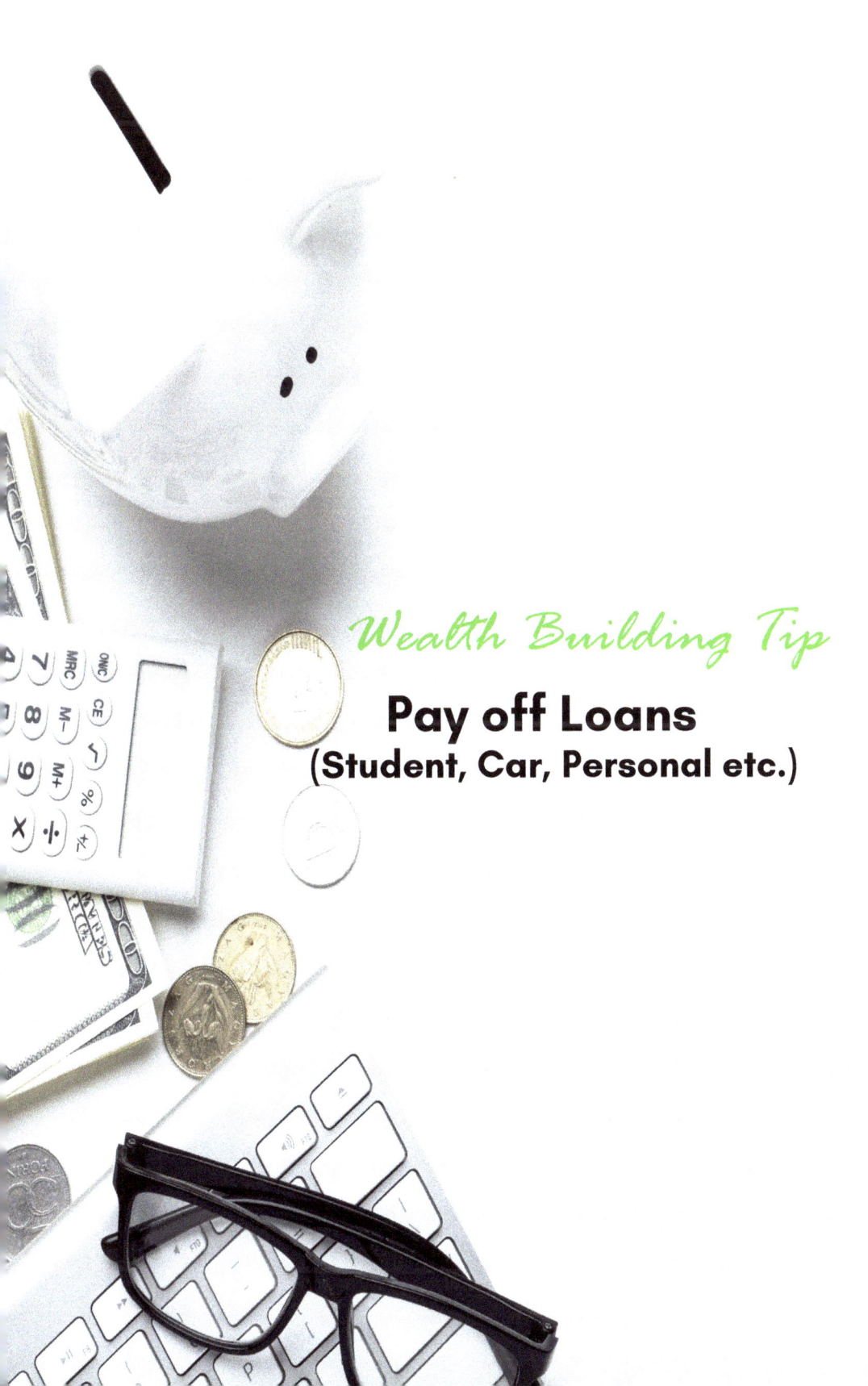

Wealth Building Tip

**Pay off Loans
(Student, Car, Personal etc.)**

Monthly Budget

Monthly Spending _____

SUN	MON	TUE	WED	THU	FRI	SAT

BILL AND EXPENSE TRACKER

Monthly Bill Checklist _____

- ☐ _____
- ☐ _____
- ☐ _____
- ☐ _____
- ☐ _____

- ☐ _____
- ☐ _____
- ☐ _____
- ☐ _____
- ☐ _____

BILLS PAID _____

BILLS DUE _____

PURCHASE TRACKER

ITEM PURCHASED	STORE	AMOUNT

ITEM PURCHASED	STORE	AMOUNT

Write & Recite:

My finances improve Daily

_____

_____

What is my relationship and thoughts about money?
(Journal your relationship with Money Here)

A billion here, a billion there, and pretty soon you're talking about real money.

Everett Dirksen

Monthly Wealth Checklist

How much money do I have in my Checking Account?

[ ]

How much money do I want in my Checking Account by the end of the month?

[ ]

How much money do I have in my Savings Account?

[ ]

How much money do I want in my Savings Account by the end of the month?

[ ]

How much money do I want in my Retirement Account by the end of the month?

[ ]

Wealth Building Tip

Pay off high interest debt

Monthly Budget

Monthly Spending _____

SUN	MON	TUE	WED	THU	FRI	SAT

BILL AND EXPENSE TRACKER

Monthly Bill Checklist _____

- ☐ _____
- ☐ _____
- ☐ _____
- ☐ _____
- ☐ _____

- ☐ _____
- ☐ _____
- ☐ _____
- ☐ _____
- ☐ _____

BILLS PAID _____

BILLS DUE _____

PURCHASE TRACKER

ITEM PURCHASED	STORE	AMOUNT

ITEM PURCHASED	STORE	AMOUNT

Write & Recite:

Money is my Friend

_____

_____

What is my relationship and thoughts about money?
(Journal your relationship with Money Here)

Do what you love and the money will follow.

Marsha Sinetar

Monthly Wealth Checklist

How much money do I have in my Checking Account?

[ ]

How much money do I want in my Checking Account by the end of the month?

[ ]

How much money do I have in my Savings Account?

[ ]

How much money do I want in my Savings Account by the end of the month?

[ ]

How much money do I want in my Retirement Account by the end of the month?

[ ]

Wealth Building Tip
Negotiate Your Salary

Monthly Budget

Monthly Spending _____

SUN	MON	TUE	WED	THU	FRI	SAT

BILL AND EXPENSE TRACKER

Monthly Bill Checklist _____

- ☐ _____
- ☐ _____
- ☐ _____
- ☐ _____
- ☐ _____

- ☐ _____
- ☐ _____
- ☐ _____
- ☐ _____
- ☐ _____

BILLS PAID _____

BILLS DUE _____

PURCHASE TRACKER

ITEM PURCHASED	STORE	AMOUNT

ITEM PURCHASED	STORE	AMOUNT

Write & Recite:
I attract Wealth

_____

_____

What is my relationship and thoughts about money?
(Journal your relationship with Money Here)

Excuse me while I save, invest, and build wealth.

Stephanie Lahart

Monthly Wealth Checklist

How much money do I have in my Checking Account?

How much money do I want in my Checking Account by the end of the month?

How much money do I have in my Savings Account?

How much money do I want in my Savings Account by the end of the month?

How much money do I want in my Retirement Account by the end of the month?

Monthly Budget

Monthly Spending _____

SUN	MON	TUE	WED	THU	FRI	SAT

BILL AND EXPENSE TRACKER

Monthly Bill Checklist _____

- ☐ _____
- ☐ _____
- ☐ _____
- ☐ _____
- ☐ _____

- ☐ _____
- ☐ _____
- ☐ _____
- ☐ _____
- ☐ _____

BILLS PAID _____

BILLS DUE _____

PURCHASE TRACKER

ITEM PURCHASED	STORE	AMOUNT		ITEM PURCHASED	STORE	AMOUNT

Write & Recite:
I am embrace new avenues of income

_____

_____

What is my relationship and thoughts about money?
(Journal your relationship with Money Here)

Networking is an Essential Part of Building Wealth.

Armstong William

Monthly Wealth Checklist

How much money do I have in my Checking Account?

[ ]

How much money do I want in my Checking Account by the end of the month?

[ ]

How much money do I have in my Savings Account?

[ ]

How much money do I want in my Savings Account by the end of the month?

[ ]

How much money do I want in my Retirement Account by the end of the month?

[ ]

Wealth Building Tip

Invest in your Education

Monthly Budget

Monthly Spending _____

SUN	MON	TUE	WED	THU	FRI	SAT

BILL AND EXPENSE TRACKER

Monthly Bill Checklist _____

- [ ] _____
- [ ] _____
- [ ] _____
- [ ] _____
- [ ] _____

- [ ] _____
- [ ] _____
- [ ] _____
- [ ] _____
- [ ] _____

BILLS PAID _____

BILLS DUE _____

PURCHASE TRACKER

ITEM PURCHASED	STORE	AMOUNT

ITEM PURCHASED	STORE	AMOUNT

Write & Recite:

I will have large amounts of money

_____

_____

What is my relationship and thoughts about money?
(Journal your relationship with Money Here)

Monthly Wealth Checklist

How much money do I have in my Checking Account?

How much money do I want in my Checking Account by the end of the month?

How much money do I have in my Savings Account?

How much money do I want in my Savings Account by the end of the month?

How much money do I want in my Retirement Account by the end of the month?

Wealth Building Tip

Carpool

Monthly Budget

Monthly Spending _____

SUN	MON	TUE	WED	THU	FRI	SAT

BILL AND EXPENSE TRACKER

Monthly Bill Checklist _____

- ☐ _____
- ☐ _____
- ☐ _____
- ☐ _____
- ☐ _____

- ☐ _____
- ☐ _____
- ☐ _____
- ☐ _____
- ☐ _____

BILLS PAID _____

BILLS DUE _____

PURCHASE TRACKER

ITEM PURCHASED	STORE	AMOUNT		ITEM PURCHASED	STORE	AMOUNT

Write & Recite:

I become richer every day

_____

_____

What is my relationship and thoughts about money?
(Journal your relationship with Money Here)

Your parents are not your emergency fund and your children are not your retirement fund. Build Your Own Wealth.

Unknown

Monthly Wealth Checklist

How much money do I have in my Checking Account?

How much money do I want in my Checking Account by the end of the month?

How much money do I have in my Savings Account?

How much money do I want in my Savings Account by the end of the month?

How much money do I want in my Retirement Account by the end of the month?

Wealth Building Tip

Get rid of subscriptions
(Amazon Prime, Hulu, Netflix etc.)

Monthly Budget

Monthly Spending _____

SUN	MON	TUE	WED	THU	FRI	SAT

BILL AND EXPENSE TRACKER

Monthly Bill Checklist _____

- ☐ _____
- ☐ _____
- ☐ _____
- ☐ _____
- ☐ _____

- ☐ _____
- ☐ _____
- ☐ _____
- ☐ _____
- ☐ _____

BILLS PAID _____

BILLS DUE _____

PURCHASE TRACKER

ITEM PURCHASED	STORE	AMOUNT		ITEM PURCHASED	STORE	AMOUNT

Write & Recite:

I always have more than enough money

_____

_____

What is my relationship and thoughts about money?
(Journal your relationship with Money Here)

If you hang with 2 millionaires you will be the 3rd.

Unknown

Monthly Wealth Checklist

How much money do I have in my Checking Account?

[ ]

How much money do I want in my Checking Account by the end of the month?

[ ]

How much money do I have in my Savings Account?

[ ]

How much money do I want in my Savings Account by the end of the month?

[ ]

How much money do I want in my Retirement Account by the end of the month?

[ ]

Wealth Building Tip

Start a Business

Monthly Budget

Monthly Spending _____

SUN	MON	TUE	WED	THU	FRI	SAT

BILL AND EXPENSE TRACKER

Monthly Bill Checklist _____

- ☐ _____
- ☐ _____
- ☐ _____
- ☐ _____
- ☐ _____

- ☐ _____
- ☐ _____
- ☐ _____
- ☐ _____
- ☐ _____

BILLS PAID _____

BILLS DUE _____

PURCHASE TRACKER

ITEM PURCHASED	STORE	AMOUNT

ITEM PURCHASED	STORE	AMOUNT

Write & Recite:

I am Prosperous

_____

_____

What is my relationship and thoughts about money?
(Journal your relationship with Money Here)

You aren't wealthy until you have something money can't buy.

Neil Armstong

Monthly Wealth Checklist

How much money do I have in my Checking Account?

[ ]

How much money do I want in my Checking Account by the end of the month?

[ ]

How much money do I have in my Savings Account?

[ ]

How much money do I want in my Savings Account by the end of the month?

[ ]

How much money do I want in my Retirement Account by the end of the month?

[ ]

Wealth Building Tip

**Remember 50/30/20 rule.
Live off of 50%, Keep 30% for variable expenses and invest 20%.
(seek investment expert for this)**

Monthly Budget

Monthly Spending _____

SUN	MON	TUE	WED	THU	FRI	SAT

BILL AND EXPENSE TRACKER

Monthly Bill Checklist _____

- ☐ _____
- ☐ _____
- ☐ _____
- ☐ _____
- ☐ _____

- ☐ _____
- ☐ _____
- ☐ _____
- ☐ _____
- ☐ _____

BILLS PAID _____

BILLS DUE _____

PURCHASE TRACKER

ITEM PURCHASED	STORE	AMOUNT

ITEM PURCHASED	STORE	AMOUNT

Write & Recite:
I am Successful

_____

_____

What is my relationship and thoughts about money?
(Journal your relationship with Money Here)

The very firs t step to building wealth is
to spend less than you make.

Brian Koslow

What is my relationship and thoughts about money?
(Journal your relationship with Money Here)

What is my relationship and thoughts about money?
(Journal your relationship with Money Here)

What is my relationship and thoughts about money?
(Journal your relationship with Money Here)

What is my relationship and thoughts about money?
(Journal your relationship with Money Here)

What is my relationship and thoughts about money?
(Journal your relationship with Money Here)

What is my relationship and thoughts about money?
(Journal your relationship with Money Here)

What is my relationship and thoughts about money?
(Journal your relationship with Money Here)

What is my relationship and thoughts about money?
(Journal your relationship with Money Here)

_____
_____
_____
_____
_____
_____
_____
_____
_____
_____
_____
_____
_____
_____
_____
_____
_____
_____
_____
_____
_____
_____
_____
_____
_____
_____
_____
_____
_____

What is my relationship and thoughts about money?
(Journal your relationship with Money Here)

What is my relationship and thoughts about money?
(Journal your relationship with Money Here)

What is my relationship and thoughts about money?
(Journal your relationship with Money Here)

What is my relationship and thoughts about money?
(Journal your relationship with Money Here)

What is my relationship and thoughts about money?
(Journal your relationship with Money Here)

What is my relationship and thoughts about money?
(Journal your relationship with Money Here)

What is my relationship and thoughts about money?
(Journal your relationship with Money Here)

What is my relationship and thoughts about money?
(Journal your relationship with Money Here)

What is my relationship and thoughts about money?
(Journal your relationship with Money Here)

What is my relationship and thoughts about money?
(Journal your relationship with Money Here)

What is my relationship and thoughts about money?
(Journal your relationship with Money Here)

What is my relationship and thoughts about money?
(Journal your relationship with Money Here)

_____
_____
_____
_____
_____
_____
_____
_____
_____
_____
_____
_____
_____
_____
_____
_____
_____
_____
_____
_____
_____
_____
_____
_____
_____
_____
_____
_____

What is my relationship and thoughts about money?
(Journal your relationship with Money Here)

_____
_____
_____
_____
_____
_____
_____
_____
_____
_____
_____
_____
_____
_____
_____
_____
_____
_____
_____
_____
_____
_____
_____
_____

What is my relationship and thoughts about money?
(Journal your relationship with Money Here)

What is my relationship and thoughts about money?
(Journal your relationship with Money Here)

What is my relationship and thoughts about money?
(Journal your relationship with Money Here)

What is my relationship and thoughts about money?
(Journal your relationship with Money Here)

What is my relationship and thoughts about money?
(Journal your relationship with Money Here)

_____
_____
_____
_____
_____
_____
_____
_____
_____
_____
_____
_____
_____
_____
_____
_____
_____
_____
_____
_____
_____
_____
_____
_____
_____

What is my relationship and thoughts about money?
(Journal your relationship with Money Here)

What is my relationship and thoughts about money?
(Journal your relationship with Money Here)

What is my relationship and thoughts about money?
(Journal your relationship with Money Here)

What is my relationship and thoughts about money?
(Journal your relationship with Money Here)

What is my relationship and thoughts about money?
(Journal your relationship with Money Here)

Interested in Writing and or Publishing Your Own Book or Journal visit:
www.a2zbookspublishing.net

www.ingramcontent.com/pod-product-compliance
Lightning Source LLC
Chambersburg PA
CBHW041325110526
44592CB00021B/2822